Seattle Seahawks Trivia Quiz Book

500 Questions on All Things Blue, Green and Grey

Chris Bradshaw

Front cover image created by headfuzz by grimboid. Check out his fantastic selection of sports, music, TV and movie posters online at:

https://www.etsy.com/shop/headfuzzbygrimboid

Introduction

Think you know about the Seattle Seahawks? Put your knowledge to the test with this selection of quizzes on all things blue, green and grey.

The book covers the whole history of the franchise, from the early days at the Kingdome through to the World Championship era of Pete Carroll, Russell Wilson and the Legion of Boom.

The biggest names in Seahawks history are present and correct so look out for questions on Steve Largent, Shaun Alexander, Curt Warner, Walter Jones, Cortez Kennedy, Marshawn Lynch, Dave Krieg and many, many more.

There are 500 questions in all covering running backs and receivers, coaches and quarterbacks, pass rushers and punters and much else besides.

Each quiz contains a selection of 20 questions and is either a mixed bag of pot luck testers or is centered on a specific category such as the 1990s or defense.

There are easy, medium and hard questions offering something for novices as well as students of Seahawks history.

You'll find the answers to each quiz below the bottom of the following quiz. For example, the answers to Quiz 1: 2013 World Champions, are underneath Quiz 2: Pot Luck. The only exception is Quiz 25: Anagrams. The answers to these can be found under the Quiz 1 questions.

All statistics and records relate to the regular season unless otherwise stated. Information is correct up to the start of the 2017 season.

We hope you enjoy the Seattle Seahawks Trivia Quiz Book.

About the Author

Chris Bradshaw has written 16 quiz books including titles for Britain's biggest selling daily newspaper, The Sun, and The Times (of London). In addition to the NFL, he has written extensively on soccer, cricket, darts and poker.

He lives in Birmingham, England and has been following the NFL for over 30 years.

Acknowledgements

Many thanks to Ken and Veronica Bradshaw, Heidi Grant, Steph, James, Ben and Will Roe and Graham Nash.

CONTENTS

Quiz 1: 2013 World Champions

1. Which team did the Seahawks defeat in Super Bowl XLVIII?

2. What was the score in the big game?

3. The Seahawks defeated which two teams in the NFC Divisional and Conference Championship games?

4. Seattle opened the scoring in Super Bowl XLVIII with a safety from which defensive lineman?

5. Who returned an interception 69 yards for a touchdown in Super Bowl XLVIII?

6. Super Bowl XLVIII was hosted at which stadium?

7. Who returned the second half kick-off for an 87-yard touchdown?

8. Which two Seahawks caught touchdown passes in Super Bowl XLVIII?

9. Who surprisingly led the Seahawks in rushing in Super Bowl XLVIII with 45 yards?

10. Which defensive lineman was the only Seahawk to record a sack in Super Bowl XLVIII?

11. Who became only the third linebacker in NFL history to be named Super Bowl MVP?

12. Who scored the Seahawks' only rushing touchdown in Super Bowl XLVIII?

13. Which Super Bowl-winning quarterback performed the coin toss?

14. True or false – Nobody on the Seattle roster had previously appeared in a Super Bowl?

15. Which Seahawks lineman sported an enormous beard at Super Bowl XLVIII having not shaved since the previous July?

16. Who was the referee of Super Bowl XLVIII?

17. Which band appeared alongside Bruno Mars during the half-time show?

18. Which soprano sang the national anthem prior to the game?

19. How many yards did Russell Wilson throw for in Super Bowl XLVIII? a) 206 b) 256 c) 306

20. What color jerseys did the Seahawks wear? a) blue b) grey c) white

Quiz 25: Answers

1. Russell Wilson 2. Richard Sherman 3. Walter Jones 4. Curt Warner 5. Earl Thomas 6. Steve Largent 7. Pete Carroll 8. Kam Chancellor 9. Matt Hasselbeck 10. Dave Krieg 11. Cortez Kennedy 12. Doug Baldwin 13. Bobby Wagner 14. Michael Bennett 15. Chris Warren 16. Max Unger 17. Fredd Young 18. Steven Hauschka 19. Shaun Alexander 20. Brian Blades

Quiz 2: Pot Luck

1. Who led the Seahawks in receiving every year from 1976 through to 1987?

2. In which year did the Seahawks make their NFL debut?

3. How did Notre Dame defensive tackle Steve Niehaus become a unique part of Seattle history in 1976?

4. The Seahawks played a 'Color Rush' game against the Rams in 2016 wearing what color uniform?

5. Which Seahawks receiver has starred in a series of YouTube videos titled 'Fresh Files'?

6. What number jersey has the franchise retired to honor Seahawks fans?

7. In October 2016 the Seahawks were involved in an amazing 6-6 tie with which team?

8. What is the name of the Seahawks cheerleading team?

9. True or false – The Seahawks are the only NFL team to have played in both the AFC and the NFC Championship game?

10. Which former Seahawk was the first officially deaf offensive player in NFL history?

11. Who is the only Seahawk to have been named a First-Team All-Pro on four occasions?

12. Seahawks owner Paul Allen was the co-founder of which giant technology company?

13. Is the field at CenturyLink Field grass or artificial turf?

14. Who was the first Seattle coach to win the AP NFL Coach of the Year award?

15. Who are the three Seahawks wide receivers with over 1,000 receiving yards and double-digit touchdowns in the same season?

16. Up to and including the 2016 season, how many head coaches had Seattle had in the history of the franchise?

17. Which long-time Seahawks kicker had the nickname 'Mr Automatic'?

18. True or false – Between 2005 and 2015 the Seahawks were a perfect 10-0 and Monday Night games?

19. What is the official color of the Seahawks' home jersey? a) college navy b) school navy c) university navy

20. Marshawn Lynch is a noted connoisseur of which candy? a) Maltesers b) M&Ms c) Skittles

Quiz 1: Answers

1. Denver Broncos 2. 43-8 3. New Orleans and San Francisco 4. Cliff Avril 5. Malcolm Smith 6. MetLife Stadium 7. Percy Harvin 8. Doug Baldwin and Jermaine Kearse 9. Percy Harvin 10. Chris Clemons 11. Malcolm Smith 12. Marshawn Lynch 13. Joe Namath 14. True 15. Max Unger 16. Terry McAulay 17. Red Hot Chili Peppers 18. Renée Fleming 19. a) 206 20. c) White

Quiz 3: Russell Wilson

1. What number jersey does Wilson wear?

2. The Seahawks selected Wilson in which round of the NFL draft?

3. Wilson spent his final year of college at which school?

4. Before transferring in his final year, Wilson started 50 games at quarterback for which college?

5. True or false – Wilson's middle name is Ewing?

6. Wilson holds the record for the most passing yards by a Seattle rookie. Who was the previous holder of that record?

7. True or false – Wilson won his first 10 starts against teams that featured a Super Bowl-winning quarterback?

8. Wilson threw his first NFL touchdown against the Cardinals in 2012. Which wide receiver caught it?

9. Wilson is one of three quarterbacks to have thrown over 50 touchdowns in his first two NFL seasons. Who are the other two?

10. Wilson's longest run was a franchise record 55-yard effort against which divisional rival in December 2014?

11. In 2012 and 2013 Wilson became only the second quarterback in NFL history to throw for over 50 TDs and rush for over 1,000 yards in a two-year period. Who was the first player to do it?

12. Wilson scored a hat-trick of rushing touchdowns during a December 2012 win at which AFC team?

13. True or false – Wilson holds the record for the most regular season wins by a starting quarterback in his first four seasons in the NFL?

14. Which baseball team drafted Wilson in the 4th round of the 2010 MLB draft?

15. Wilson was a former roommate of which baseball World Series MVP?

16. Wilson threw five touchdown passes in a game twice in the space of three weeks in 2015. Against which two AFC teams did he throw them?

17. In a 2016 game against the Eagles, Wilson caught his first touchdown pass. Which wide receiver threw it?

18. Wilson married which singer in 2016?

19. Wilson tied the record for the most touchdowns thrown by a quarterback in their rookie season. With whom does he share that record? a) Tom Brady b) Eli Manning c) Peyton Manning

20. How many touchdowns did Wilson throw in that historic rookie year? a) 24 b) 25 c) 26

Quiz 2: Answers

1. Steve Largent 2. 1976 3. He was the first player selected by Seattle in the NFL Draft 4. Green 5. Doug Baldwin 6. #12 7. Arizona 8. The Sea Gals 9. True 10. Derrick Coleman 11. Walter Jones 12. Microsoft 13. Artificial turf 14. Jack Patera 15. Steve Largent, Joey Galloway and Doug Baldwin 16. Eight 17. Norm Johnson 18. True 19. a) College navy 20. c) Skittles

Quiz 4: Pot Luck

1. Seattle destroyed which division rival 58-0 in December 2014, securing the biggest win in franchise history?

2. Which running back holds the record for the most rushing yards in the playoffs in franchise history?

3. In 1986, Steve Largent caught his 751st pass to become the NFL's all-time leading receiver. Which former Charger and Bengal previously held that record?

4. Up to the start of the 2017 season, who was the only Seahawks head coach to feature on the team's Ring of Honor?

5. Which hard-hitting Seattle defensive back was inducted into the Pro Football Hall of Fame in 2017?

6. True or false – The Seahawks didn't have a single first round pick in the 2013, 2014 or 2015 NFL Draft?

7. In November 2013, the Seahawks overturned a record 21-point deficit, eventually going on to beat which team 27-24 in overtime?

8. True or false – In their first season in the NFL the Seahawks players wore black shoes?

9. Up to the start of the 2017 season, only one Seahawk had won the AP NFL Player of the Year award. Which one?

10. Which original Seahawk has been the play-by-play radio announcer on Seattle games since the early 2000s?

11. Which Hall of Fame quarterback is a regular member of the Seahawks radio commentary team?

12. Which ten-year Seahawks linebacker was named defensive coordinator of the Pittsburgh Steelers in 2015?

13. Up to the start of the 2017 season the Seahawks had a perfect 3-0 playoff record against which NFC rival?

14. What does the K in the name of K.J. Wright stand for?

15. In 1986, the Seahawks rushed for a mammoth 298 yards in a 41-16 victory over which eventual AFC champion?

16. Who played the most offensive snaps during the 2013 World Championship-winning season?

17. Who played the most defensive snaps during the 2013 World Championship-winning season?

18. The longest losing streak in franchise history ran for how many games?

19. What is the highest number of points the Seahawks have scored in a single regular season? a) 418 b) 423 c) 452

20. Marshawn Lynch came out of retirement and left the Seahawks for which team? a) Denver b) Kansas City c) Oakland

Quiz 3: Answers

1. #3 2. Third 3. University of Wisconsin 4. North Carolina State 5. False 6. Rick Mirer 7. True 8. Sidney Rice 9. Dan Marino and Peyton Manning 10. Arizona 11. Randall Cunningham 12. Buffalo 13. True 14. Colorado Rockies 15. Madison Bumgarner 16. Pittsburgh and Baltimore 17. Doug Baldwin 18. Ciara 19. c) Peyton Manning 20. c) 26

Quiz 5: Pete Carroll

1. In what year did Pete Carroll become the head coach of the Seahawks?

2. Prior to taking the helm in Seattle, Carroll was the head coach at which college?

3. In 1994, Carroll spent a single season as head coach of which NFL team?

4. The Seahawks had the same win loss record in Carroll's first two seasons in Seattle. What was it?

5. Between 1997 and 1999 Carroll was the head coach of which AFC team?

6. Whom did Carroll succeed as the Seahawks head coach?

7. Carroll's first postseason victory with the Seahawks was a shock 41-36 win over which team?

8. In 1995 and 1996 Carroll was the defensive coordinator at which NFC rival?

9. True or false – At college, Coach Carroll had the nickname 'Big Balls Pete'?

10. Carroll is one of only three head coaches to win a Super Bowl and a College National Championship. Who are the other two?

11. True or false – Coach Carroll was the oldest head coach in the NFL during the 2016 season?

12. Coach Carroll played college ball at which school?

13. What position did he play during his college football career?

14. Carroll started his NFL coaching career with a brief spell as defensive backs coach at which AFC East team?

15. What is the most wins the Seahawks have recorded in a single regular season under Coach Carroll?

16. True or false – The Seahawks have reached the plays-offs every year since Carroll became head coach?

17. In the mid-1980s Carroll spent five years as a defensive backs coach with which NFC North franchise?

18. Coach Carroll was born and brought up in which state?

19. What is the title of Coach Carroll's 2010 book? a) Win Now b) Win Forever c) Win Together

20. How old was Coach Carroll when he became the head coach of the Seahawks? a) 55 b) 57 c) 59

Quiz 4: Answers

1. Arizona 2. Marshawn Lynch 3. Charlie Joiner 4. Chuck Knox 5. Kenny Easley 6. True 7. Tampa Bay 8. True 9. Shaun Alexander 10. Steve Raible 11. Warren Moon 12. Keith Butler 13. Washington 14. Kenneth 15. Denver 16. Russell Wilson 17. Earl Thomas 18. 10 19. c) 452 20. c) Oakland

Quiz 6: Pot Luck

1. The Seahawks drafted star running back Shaun Alexander from which college?

2. Which 2017 draft pick shares a name with a former world heavyweight boxing champion?

3. What is the name of the Major League Soccer franchise that shares CenturyLink Field with the Seahawks?

4. Who is the only Seahawk receiver to have had his jersey number retired?

5. Matt Hasselbeck threw a postseason franchise record four touchdown passes during a famous wild card win over which team?

6. Which expansion team entered the NFL in the same year as the Seahawks?

7. True or false – Marshawn Lynch makes a cameo appearance in the video game 'Call of Duty: Black Ops III'?

8. Which quarterback holds the record for the most fumbles in franchise history?

9. Of players with over 400 rushing attempts, who has the best yards per carry average?

10. Three players threw touchdown passes during the 2016 regular season. Russell Wilson was one. Who were the other two?

11. Which Seahawks linebacker, who was with the team from 1997 through to 2004, is the owner of an online newspaper called The Reptile Report?

12. Which member of the Seahawks' Super Bowl XLVIII-winning roster had previously won Canada's Grey Cup in 2008?

13. Which controversial linebacker did the Seahawks select with the 22nd pick of the 1988 NFL draft?

14. True or false – The Seahawks' logo is based on a mask created by the Kwakwaka'wakw tribe?

15. In 2005, who became the first Seahawks center to be named to the Pro Bowl?

16. What is the name of the drumline that performs by the 12th Man Flag at Seattle home games?

17. What is the name of the family who were the original owners of the Seahawks franchise?

18. The Seahawks scored a record 31 points in the second quarter during a 48-23 rout of which NFC rival in 2002?

19. In which year of their history did the Seahawks record their first winning season? a) 1st b) 2nd c) 3rd

20. Between 2012 and 2013 Marshawn Lynch rushed for a touchdown in how many successive playoff games? a) 4 b) 5 c) 6

Quiz 5: Answers

1. 2010 2. USC 3. New York Jets 4. 7-9 5. New England 6. Jim Mora Jr 7. New Orleans 8. San Francisco 9. True 10. Jimmy Johnson and Barry Switzer 11. True 12. Pacific University 13. Safety 14. Buffalo 15. 13 wins 16. False 17. Minnesota Vikings 18. California 19. b) Win Forever 20. c) 59

Quiz 7: Quarterbacks

1. Who is Seattle's all-time leader in passing yards with 29,434?

2. Who holds the record for the most touchdown passes in franchise history with 195?

3. Who is the only Seattle quarterback to throw for over 4,000 yards in a single season?

4. Which Hall of Fame-quarterback threw for 36 touchdowns during a brief stint in Seattle in the late 1990s?

5. Whose 90-yard touchdown pass against the Eagles in 2008 is the longest in franchise history?

6. Of Seahawk quarterbacks with 30 or more starts, only four have a better than .500 record. Name the quartet.

7. Which lefty played 126 games for the Seahawks between 1976 and 1984?

8. Seattle has twice used a first-round draft pick on a quarterback. Who did they take in 1991 and 1993 respectively?

9. Which Super Bowl-winning quarterback had a starting record of eight wins and four defeats in a spell in Seattle that stretched from 2001 to 2004?

10. Which quarterback has been sacked the most times in franchise history?

11. Russell Wilson threw three touchdown-passes in playoff games against which NFC rival in both 2015 and 2016?

12. Who holds the franchise record for throwing the most interceptions in a single season?

13. Which one-time Seattle quarterback has the nickname 'Clipboard Jesus'?

14. Who was the back-up quarterback on Seattle's Super Bowl XLVIII roster?

15. Who are the five Seahawks quarterbacks with 20 or more regular season wins?

16. Which quarterback won his one and only start for the Seahawks, beating Chicago 14-13 in September 1999?

17. Who holds the record for the most passes intercepted in franchise history with 148?

18. Of players with over 500 passing attempts, Russell Wilson has the top passer rating. Who, somewhat surprisingly, is second on the list?

19. Between 1983 and 1985 Dave Krieg threw touchdown passes in how many consecutive games? a) 27 b) 28 c) 29

20. In 2015, Russell Wilson set the franchise record for the most touchdown passes thrown in a single regular season. How many did he throw? a) 34 b) 35 c) 36

Quiz 6: Answers

1. Alabama 2. Mike Tyson 3. Seattle Sounders 4. Steve Largent 5. New Orleans 6. Tampa Bay 7. True 8. Dave Krieg 9. Russell Wilson 10. Doug Baldwin and Trevone Boykin 11. Chad Brown 12. Brandon Browner 13. Brian Bosworth 14. True 15. Robbie Tobeck 16. Blue Thunder 17. Nordstrom 18. Minnesota 19. c) 3rd 20. b) 5

Quiz 8: Pot Luck

1. Who was the first player to be honored on the Seahawks Ring of Honor?

2. Which former Seahawks special teams star is now a wine producer whose labels include a red called 'Loud and Proud'?

3. Which defensive star was the Seahawks' emergency quarterback in 2016?

4. The Seahawks reached the Conference Championship game for the first time under the stewardship of which head coach?

5. Up to the close of the 2016 season, only three Seahawks quarterbacks had thrown for over 400 yards in a game. Can you name the trio?

6. In 2011, which Seahawk became the first undrafted rookie to lead his team in both receptions and receiving yards in the Super Bowl era?

7. Which Seahawk appeared on the cover of the Madden 2015 video game?

8. True or false – The Seahawks scored a touchdown in 57 successive games between 2012 and 2015?

9. Which member of Seattle's 2013 Super Bowl winning roster played for the Patriots against the Seahawks in Super Bowl XLIX?

10. Who is the only player in franchise history whose surname starts with the letter Z?

11. Who is the only Seahawks offensive lineman to have had his jersey number retired?

12. What number jersey is worn by the Seahawks mascot?

13. On the current Seahawks helmet, what two colors make up the bird's eye?

14. Legendary wide receiver Steve Largent arrived in Seattle following a trade with which team?

15. The Seahawks gave up a pick in which round of the 1976 Draft to acquire the services of Largent?

16. True or false – The Seahawks weren't involved in a tied game until 2016?

17. Which kicker holds the record for the most consecutive successful field goals in Seahawks history?

18. Who holds the franchise record for the most passing yards in a single game?

19. How many times in his Seahawks career did Dave Krieg fumble? a) 88 b) 98 c) 108

20. What is the official name of the shade of green that appears on Seattle's uniform? a) action green b) battle green c) combat green

Quiz 7: Answers

1. Matt Hasselbeck 2. Dave Krieg 3. Russell Wilson 4. Warren Moon 5. Seneca Wallace 6. Wilson, Krieg, Hasselbeck and Jon Kitna 7. Jim Zorn 8. Dan McGwire and Rick Mirer 9. Trent Dilfer 10. Dave Krieg 11. Carolina 12. Jim Zorn 13. Charlie Whitehurst 14. Tarvaris Jackson 15. Wilson, Hasselbeck, Krieg, Zorn and Mirer 16. Glenn Foley 17. Dave Krieg 18. Seneca Wallace 19. b) 28 20. a) 34

Quiz 9: Running Backs

1. With 9,429 yards, who is Seattle's all-time leading rusher?

2. 'Beast Mode' was the nickname of which Seattle back?

3. Who set the franchise record for the most rushing yards in a postseason game after amassing 161 yards against the Lions in January 2017?

4. Who led the Seahawks in rushing in 2016, despite amassing just 491 yards?

5. In 2010, the Seahawks traded two draft picks with which team to acquire the services of Marshawn Lynch?

6. Who is the only Seahawk aged over 30 to have rushed for over 1,000 yards in a season?

7. What does the C in the name C.J. Prosise stand for?

8. Who led the team in rushing for six successive years 1992 to 1997?

9. Which full back rushed for 4,579 yards during a Seahawks career that ran from 1986 through to 1993?

10. The Seahawks last used a first-round draft pick on a running back in 2001. Who did they select?

11. Which Seattle back rushed for over 1,000 yards in 1983, 1985, 1986 and 1988?

12. Which former Philadelphia Eagle rushed for 4,009 yards during a four-year stint in Seattle between 1998 and 2001?

13. The longest run by a Seahawk in the playoffs was a memorable 67-yard touchdown dash from Marshawn Lynch in January 2011 against which team?

14. Which Seattle full back was named a First-Team All-Pro in 2005?

15. In a 2012 game against Arizona, two Seahawks running backs rushed for over 100 yards. Marshawn Lynch was one. Who was the other?

16. Shaun Alexander holds the record for the most rushing touchdowns in franchise history. Who is second on the list?

17. Which alliteratively named back led the Seahawks in rushing in both 2008 and 2009?

18. Who is the only Seahawk to win the NFL rushing title?

19. What is the longest run in franchise history? a) 86 yards b) 87 yards c) 88 yards

20. Shaun Alexander holds the NFL record for the most rushing touchdowns in a single season. How many did he score in 2005? a) 25 b) 26 c) 27

Quiz 8: Answers

1. Steve Largent 2. Norm Johnson 3. Kam Chancellor 4. Chuck Knox 5. Matt Hasselbeck, Dave Krieg and Warren Moon 6. Doug Baldwin 7. Richard Sherman 8. True 9. Brandon Browner 10. Jim Zorn 11. Walter Jones 12. 0 13. Green and blue 14. Houston Oilers 15. 8th 16. True 17. Olindo Mare 18. Matt Hasselbeck 19. c) 108 20. a) Action green

Quiz 10: Pot Luck

1. Who was the offensive coordinator on Seattle's 2013 Super Bowl-winning team?

2. The Seahawks played their first overseas game in 1990 in which Asian city?

3. Which team did they face in that historic game?

4. Who was the first career-Seahawks player elected to the Pro Football Hall of Fame?

5. Which Seahawks player has made the most Pro Bowl appearances in franchise history?

6. True or false – Long-time Seahawks quarterback Matt Hasselbeck has been struck by lightning?

7. Which former Oakland head coach was appointed the Seahawks' offensive line coach in 2011?

8. In which round of the 2010 NFL Draft did the Seahawks select star safety Kam Chancellor?

9. Who kicked a field goal in 14 consecutive games in 2011 and 2012 to set a new franchise record?

10. The Seahawks' first ever regular season victory was a 13-10 over which team?

11. A player from which visiting team was sued after a snowball fight broke out in a 2008 game at Century Link Field?

12. True or false – The Seahawks were originally going to be named the Stallions?

13. Which Seahawks running back has the Twitter handle @Lil_Eazy_Ana_42?

14. Who are the three Seattle quarterbacks to have thrown over 20 interceptions in a single season?

15. Who is the only Seahawk to have won the Walter Payton NFL Man of the Year Award?

16. Which former Seahawk is the anchor on KIRO 7 Eyewitness News?

17. The longest home losing streak in franchise history stretched to how many games?

18. Which Seahawks linebacker spent four seasons in Seattle between 1984 and 1987 and went to the Pro Bowl every year?

19. Up to the start of the 2017 season the Seahawks had won how many games in franchise history (including playoffs)? a) 281 b) 321 c) 341

20. The Seahawks hold the NFL record for the fewest net yards gained in a single game. How many did they collect against the Rams in November 1979? a) -7 b) 7 c) 17

Quiz 9: Answers

1. Shaun Alexander 2. Marshawn Lynch 3. Thomas Rawls 4. Christine Michael 5. Buffalo 6. Ricky Watters 7. Calvin 8. Chris Warren 9. John L. Williams 10. Shaun Alexander 11. Curt Warner 12. Ricky Watters 13. New Orleans 14. Mack Strong 15. Robert Turbin 16. Marshawn Lynch 17. Julius Jones 18. Shaun Alexander 19. c) 88 yards 20. c) 27

Quiz 11: Receivers

1. With 13,089 yards who is the Seahawks' all-time leading receiver?

2. Who tied the franchise record for the most receptions in a season in 2016 after grabbing 94 passes?

3. Which receiver set the original record of 94 catches during the 2007 season?

4. The Seahawks acquired tight end Jimmy Graham from which team?

5. In a wild win over the Chargers in 1985, who became the first Seahawk with four touchdown receptions in a single game?

6. Which Seahawk tied for the League lead with 14 touchdown receptions in 2015?

7. The Seahawks have used a first-round draft pick on a wide receiver twice. Which two players did they select in 1995 and 2001?

8. With 471 career catches, who has been Seattle's most prolific running back in the passing game?

9. With 64 catches for 898 yards, who led the Seahawks in receiving in the 2013 World Championship season?

10. Up to the close of the 2016 season, who was the only Seattle receiver to have had multiple 80-catch seasons?

11. Who holds the record for the most receiving yards in the postseason in Seahawks history?

12. Who caught 55 passes in 2008, the most by a rookie tight end in franchise history?

13. Steve Largent holds the record for the most touchdown receptions in franchise history. Who is second on the list?

14. In 2002, the Seahawks selected a tight end with their first-round draft pick for the first and so far, only, time. Who did they select?

15. Of players with over 100 career catches, who has the highest average per reception with 18.53 yards?

16. Which speedy receiver's 90-yard touchdown catch against the Eagles in 2008 is the longest in franchise history?

17. Steve Largent is one of just two Seattle receivers with over 500 career catches. Who is the other?

18. In 1995, who became the first and so far, only, Seahawk with over 1,000 receiving yards in his rookie season?

19. Steve Largent holds the franchise record for the most receiving yards in a single game. How many did he rack up against the Lions in 1987? a) 241 b) 251 c) 261

20. Steve Largent caught a pass in how many consecutive games? a) 157 b) 167 c) 177

Quiz 10: Answers

1. Darrell Bevell 2. Tokyo 3. Denver 4. Steve Largent 5. Walter Jones 6. True 7. Tom Cable 8. Fifth 9. Steven Hauschka 10. Tampa Bay 11. New York Jets 12. False 13. Eddie Lacy 14. Dave Krieg, Jim Zorn and Rick Mirer 15. Steve Largent 16. Steve Raible 17. 8 18. Fredd Young 19. c) 341 20. a) -7

Quiz 12: Pot Luck

1. In 1991, which quarterback became the second player inducted to the Seahawks Ring of Honor?

2. Who is the only Seahawks defender to have been elected to the Pro Bowl eight times?

3. True or false – Pete Carroll is the only head coach in franchise history with a winning postseason record?

4. What color is the facemask on the current Seahawks helmet?

5. In 2013 and 2014, the Seahawks defense led the league in points and yards allowed. What was the last team to top both categories in consecutive seasons?

6. Who are the three Seattle backs to have rushed for more than 1,500 yards in a season?

7. Which two-time Super Bowl-winning head coach had a largely unsuccessful spell in charge in Seattle between 1992 and 1994?

8. After a stellar career in Seattle, running back Shaun Alexander had a brief stint with which team?

9. Which defensive back set a club record against the Cardinals in November 2015 after recording 19 tackles?

10. True or false – In the whole of the 1992 season the Seahawks threw for just nine touchdowns?

11. The longest winning streak in Seahawks' history stretched to how many games?

12. Up to and including the 2016 season, did the Seahawks have a winning or losing playoff record?

30

13. In the Seahawks' first season in the NFL the League was made up of how many teams?

14. True or false – Running back Thomas Rawls is the grandson of the soul singer Lou Rawls?

15. Which Seahawks quarterback holds the franchise record for the most passing yards in a single playoff game?

16. In 2015, which Seahawk became only the second player in NFL history with at least five receiving touchdowns plus kickoff return and punt return touchdowns in the same season?

17. Which former Chicago Bear is the only other player to manage the feat from Q16?

18. The last ever game played at the Kingdome was a 20-17 playoff loss to which team?

19. What is the official name of the shade of grey that appears on the Seahawks uniform? a) hawk grey b) seal grey c) wolf grey

20. How many wins did the Seahawks record in their first season in the NFL? a) 1 b) 2 c) 3

Quiz 11: Answers

1. Steve Largent 2. Doug Baldwin 3. Bobby Engram 4. New Orleans 5. Daryl Turner 6. Doug Baldwin 7. Joey Galloway and Koren Robinson 8. John L. Williams 9. Golden Tate 10. Brian Blades 11. Doug Baldwin 12. John Carlson 13. Darrell Jackson 14. Jerramy Stevens 15. Daryl Turner 16. Koren Robinson 17. Brian Blades 18. Joey Galloway 19. c) 261 20. c) 177

Quiz 13: Defense

1. By what nickname is Seattle's defensive backfield collectively known?

2. Who was the Seattle defensive coordinator during the 2013 World Championship winning season?

3. Who is the only Seahawks defender to have had his jersey number retired?

4. True or false – The Seahawks once allowed over 350 rushing yards in a single game?

5. Which Seahawk led the NFL in tackles in 2016?

6. Which defensive back, who spent a decade in Seattle in the late 1980s and early 1990s, is the Seahawks' all-time leader in tackles?

7. In a 1984 game against the Chiefs, Seattle set the NFL record for the most pick-sixes in a single game. How many did they take to the house?

8. Who were the two Seahawks to record double-digit sacks during the 2016 season?

9. True or false – The Seahawks led the NFL in scoring defense for four successive years from 2012?

10. Which lineman led the team in sacks in 2013, 2014 and 2015?

11. With 218 appearances between 1982 and 1996, which defensive lineman holds the record for the most games played by a Seahawk?

12. Whose 94-yard return for a touchdown against the Giants in 2011 is the longest pick-six in Seahawks history?

13. Which linebacker, who later became an assistant coach in Seattle, led the Seahawks in tackles for four successive seasons from 2005 to 2008?

14. In 1998, who set the franchise record for the most sacks in a single season with 18.5?

15. With eight picks, who led the NFL in interceptions in 2013?

16. Who is Seattle's all-time leader in quarterback sacks, recording 116 of them between 1980 and 1991?

17. True or false – In the 2015 season finale against the Cardinals, the Seattle defense didn't give up a single rushing first down?

18. Which defensive back, who played between 1976 and 1986, recorded a franchise record 50 interceptions as a Seahawk?

19. How many touchdowns did the Seahawks defense give up during the Championship-winning 2013 season? a) 22 b) 23 c) 24

20. What is the fewest number of points that the Seattle defense has given up in a 16-game regular season? a) 231 b) 235 c) 241

Quiz 12: Answers

1. Jim Zorn 2. Cortez Kennedy 3. True 4. Blue 5. Chicago 6. Shaun Alexander, Marshawn Lynch and Chris Warren 7. Tom Flores 8. Washington 9. Kam Chancellor 10. True 11. 11 12. Winning (16-15) 13. 28 14. False 15. Russell Wilson 16. Tyler Lockett 17. Gale Sayers 18. Miami 19. c) wolf grey 20. b) 2

Quiz 14: Pot Luck

1. Between his two stints in Seattle, defensive lineman Michael Bennett had a spell with which NFC team?

2. Which guard holds the record for the most successive starts for the Seahawks with 121 between 1999 and 2006?

3. In 2001, Shaun Alexander ran for a franchise record 266 yards against which team?

4. Who was the Seahawks' head coach in their first six seasons in the NFL?

5. In 1992, which cornerback became the first defensive player inducted to the Seahawks Ring of Honor?

6. Who is the only Seahawks punter to boot over 100 punts in a single regular season?

7. Former Seahawks wide receiver and return specialist Nate Burleson was born in which country?

8. Which Michigan State defensive tackle did the Seahawks select with their first pick in the 2017 NFL Draft?

9. Full back Mack Strong blocked for which three 1,000-yard rushers?

10. Who is the only Seahawks head coach whose first name and surname start with the same letter?

11. Who are the three players in Seahawks history to have recorded more than 10 sacks in three successive seasons?

12. True or false – The Seahawks failed to win a single playoff game between 1985 and 2005?

13. Up to the start of the 2017 season, only two Seahawks had won the AP NFL Coach of the Year Award. Which two?

14. In total, how many times did the Seahawks win the AFC West title?

15. How did Don Bitterlich etch his name in franchise history against the Cardinals in September 1976?

16. In 1984, who became the first Seahawk to win the AP NFL Defensive Player of the Year award?

17. Which Seahawks receiver, who grew up on a military base, was nominated for the 2016 NFL Salute to Service Award?

18. Which back rushed for 138 yards and two touchdowns on just six carries in a 16-13 win over the Oilers in October 1997?

19. Seahawk is another name for which bird? a) eagle b) osprey c) wren

20. How many rushing touchdowns did the Seahawks give up during their record-breaking 2013 regular season? a) 3 b) 4 c) 5

Quiz 13: Answers

1. Legion of Boom 2. Dan Quinn 3. Cortez Kennedy 4. True 5. Bobby Wagner 6. Eugene Robinson 7. Four 8. Cliff Avril and Frank Clark 9. True 10. Michael Bennett 11. Joe Nash 12. Brandon Browner 13. Lofa Tatupu 14. Michael Sinclair 15. Richard Sherman 16. Jacob Green 17. True 18. Dave Brown 19. a) 22 20. a) 231

Quiz 15: Special Teams

1. Who was the kicker on the Seahawks' Super Bowl XLVIII-winning roster?

2. Who holds the record for the most kickoff return touchdowns in Seahawks history?

3. True or false – up to the start of the 2017 season, no Seahawk had scored a punt return touchdown in the playoffs?

4. Charlie Rogers is one of two Seahawks to have scored a kickoff return touchdown in the playoffs. Who is the other?

5. With 810 points, who is Seattle's all-time leading scorer?

6. Which defensive tackle tied the franchise record with eight blocked field goals between 2004 and 2010?

7. In 2005, who became the first Seattle kicker to kick over 50 PATs in a single season?

8. Who holds the record for the longest punt in franchise history after booming a 77-yarder against the 49ers in 2011?

9. In 2006 and 2007, which Seattle wide receiver returned punts against the Rams and Browns for 90 and 94-yard touchdowns?

10. Who is the only Seahawks punter to have been elected to the Pro Bowl?

11. Which Seahawk holds the franchise record for converting the most fields goals of longer than 50 yards in a single season?

12. Who holds the record for the most career punts in franchise history?

13. Who holds the record for the most punt return touchdowns in franchise history with four?

14. Which colorful-sounding defensive lineman blocked two field goals against the Browns in October 2011?

15. What is the longest field goal in Seattle franchise history?

16. Which kicker, who spent three years in Seattle between 2008 and 2010, is the owner of a classic car restoration business called Klassic Cars?

17. Who is the only Seahawks kicker to lead the NFL in single-season scoring?

18. Which diminutive running back holds the record for the most kick returns in Seahawks history with 165?

19. Which kicker holds the record for the most successful field goals in a single regular season? a) Todd Peterson b) Rian Lindell c) Steven Hauschka

20. How many field goals were made in that record-breaking season? a) 32 b) 33 c) 34

Quiz 14: Answers

1. Tampa Bay 2. Chris Gray 3. Oakland 4. Jack Patera 5. Dave Brown 6. Rick Tuten 7. Canada 8. Malik McDowell 9. Chris Warren, Ricky Watters and Shaun Alexander 10. Mike McCormack 11. Chris Clemons, Michael Sinclair and Jacob Green 12. True 13. Jack Patera and Chuck Knox 14. Twice 15. He scored the team's first ever points 16. Kenny Easley 17. Jermaine Kearse 18. Steve Broussard 19. b) osprey 20. a) 3

Quiz 16: Pot Luck

1. Who was the Seattle head coach between 1983 and 1991?

2. Which quarterback overcame a 21-3 half time deficit against the Raiders in 1997 to claim a 22-21 win in his first career start?

3. In 1999, who succeeded Dennis Erickson as the Seahawks' head coach?

4. How many points were scored in the opening quarter of Super Bowl XLIX?

5. @MosesBread72 is the Twitter handle of which Seahawks defensive star?

6. Russell Wilson is the second youngest starting quarterback to win a Super Bowl. Who is the youngest?

7. Which former Seahawks defensive back was named the team's defensive coordinator in 2015?

8. Which alliteratively named running back was the first Seahawk to rush for over 100 yards in a single game?

9. Who was the first Seahawk to play in the Pro Bowl?

10. Defensive star Cliff Avril started his NFL career with which team?

11. Which offensive lineman caught a 19-yard touchdown pass on a fake field goal in the historic NFC Championship win over Green Bay in 2014?

12. The Seahawks' first ever pre-season game was against which current NFC West rival?

13. What color were the pants in the original Seahawks uniform?

14. Before becoming Seattle's head coach, Dennis Erickson was in charge of which college program?

15. Legendary Seahawks rusher Curt Warner won All-American honors at which college?

16. 'The Enforcer' is the nickname of which Seahawks defensive back?

17. In terms of regular season winning percentage, the Seahawks have been most successful in games played in which month?

18. Which cornerback, who had two spells in Seattle from 1978-1983 and 1986-1987, holds the record for the most blocked punts in franchise history with three?

19. Up to the start of the 2017 season, how many games, including playoffs, had the Seahawks lost in their history? a) 293 b) 313 c) 333

20. The Seahawks led the NFL in interceptions in 2013. How many picks did they make? a) 27 b) 28 c) 29

Quiz 15: Answers

1. Steven Hauschka 2. Leon Washington 3. True 4. Percy Harvin 5. Norm Johnson 6. Craig Terrill 7. Josh Brown 8. Jon Ryan 9. Nate Burleson 10. Rick Tuten 11. Steven Hauschka 12. Jon Ryan 13. Joey Galloway 14. Red Bryant 15. 58 yards 16. Olindo Mare 17. Steven Hauschka 18. Steve Broussard 19. a) Todd Peterson 20. c) 34

Quiz 17: 1980s

1. Which future Hall of Fame defensive back did the Seahawks select in the first round of the 1981 draft?

2. Which defensive back led the AFC in interceptions in 1981 after picking off 10 passes?

3. The Seahawks used the third pick of the 1983 NFL draft to select which legendary running back?

4. The Seahawks gained their first ever home playoff win at the tail end of the 1983 season against which then division rival?

5. A week later the Seahawks earned their first road playoff victory. Which AFC East team did they defeat?

6. In a 1983 game against Denver, who became the first Seahawks quarterback to throw for over 400 yards in a game?

7. True or false – The Seahawks had to wait until 1984 to win their first regular season opener?

8. In 1984, who set the franchise record for the most receiving touchdowns in a rookie season with 10?

9. True or false – The Seahawks never finished bottom of their division during the 1980s?

10. Who was the only Seattle kicker to score more than 100 points in a season during the 1980s?

11. How many times did the Seahawks win the AFC West title during the 1980s?

12. Curt Warner become the first Seahawks back to rush for over 200 yards in a game in an epic 1983 win over which division rival?

13. True or false - In the season where the Seahawks reached the playoffs for the first time the team were never more than one game above or below .500 until the regular season finale?

14. Which Hall of Fame running back spent the 13th and final year of his NFL career in 1984 in Seattle?

15. Seattle lost an overtime thriller in the 1987 Wild Card round against which AFC Central team?

16. The Seahawks lost 21-13 in the Divisional Round of the 1988 playoffs to which eventual AFC champion?

17. Two wide receivers led Seattle in touchdowns in a season during the 1980s. Steve Largent was one, who was the other?

18. Which three running backs led the team in touchdowns scored in a season during the 1980s?

19. In a 1983 game against the Jets, Seattle set a franchise record by running the ball how many times? a) 53 b) 55 c) 57

20. In 1980, the Seahawks closed the season by losing how many games in a row? a) 7 b) 8 c) 9

Quiz 16: Answers

1. Chuck Knox 2. Jon Kitna 3. Mike Holmgren 4. Zero 5. Michael Bennett 6. Ben Roethlisberger 7. Kris Richard 8. Sherman Smith 9. Steve Largent 10. Detroit 11. Garry Gilliam 12. San Francisco 13. Grey 14. University of Miami 15. Penn State 16. Kam Chancellor 17. December 18. Kerry Justin 19. c) 333 20. b) 28

Quiz 18: Pot Luck

1. In 2001, Seattle traded draft picks with which team to acquire the services of quarterback Matt Hasselbeck?

2. @BigPlayCray33 is the Twitter handle of which Seahawks defensive back?

3. Seahawks legend Steve Largent played college ball at which school?

4. True or false – Russell Wilson is the shortest starting quarterback to have won a Super Bowl?

5. Who are the three head coaches in franchise history to have guided the Seahawks to the playoffs?

6. Before becoming offensive coordinator in Seattle, Darrell Bevell spent five seasons in the same post at which NFC North team?

7. True or false – Tight end Jimmy Graham holds a pilot's license and is qualified to fly stunt planes?

8. What color pants did the Seahawks wear in their Super Bowl XLVIII triumph?

9. Before becoming top man in Seattle, Chuck Knox had head coaching spells at which two NFL franchises?

10. Which quarterback had more regular season wins as a Seahawk – Dave Krieg or Matt Hasselbeck?

11. The Seahawks reached the Super Bowl for the first team after beating which team in the NFC Championship game?

12. What was the score in that historic encounter?

13. In what year did the Seahawks win their first NFC West title?

14. Which quarterback threw the first touchdown pass in franchise history?

15. Which receiver, who was in Seattle from 1976 to 1981, caught that historic pass?

16. Who was the first broadcaster to be added to the Seahawks Ring of Honor?

17. In what year did Seattle move from the AFC West to the NFC West?

18. In 2000, which Seahawk set the AFC record for the most combined punt and kickoff return yards in a season?

19. What is the name of the Seahawks' live hawk mascot? a) Naima b) Saima c) Taima

20. Who holds the record for leading the team in rushing in the most successive seasons? a) Shaun Alexander b) Marshawn Lynch c) Curt Warner

Quiz 17: Answers

1. Kenny Easley 2. John Harris 3. Curt Warner 4. Denver 5. Miami 6. Dave Krieg 7. True 8. Daryl Turner 9. False 10. Norm Johnson 11. Once 12. Kansas City 13. True 14. Franco Harris 15. Houston Oilers 16. Cincinnati 17. Daryl Turner 18. Jim Jodat, Curt Warner and John L. Williams 19. c) 57 20. c) 9

Quiz 19: 1990s

1. Name the four Seahawks head coaches from the 1990s.

2. In 1992, who became only the second Seahawk to win the AP NFL Defensive Player of the Year award?

3. Who was the only Seahawks quarterback to be selected to the Pro Bowl in the 1990s?

4. What was the name of the owner who attempted to take the Seahawks out of Seattle and move them to California?

5. Which tech billionaire bought the Seahawks franchise in 1996?

6. Which head coach had an 8-8 record in three of his four seasons in charge of the Seahawks in the 1990s?

7. The Seahawks turned a record 20-0 deficit into an epic 31-27 win over which AFC West rival in December 1995?

8. Who was the Seattle starting quarterback in that amazing comeback?

9. Which kicker's 126 field goals between 1995 and 1999 put him third on the all-time franchise record list?

10. Which running back, who was picked in the 10th round of the 1989 Draft, led the AFC with 15 touchdowns in 1990?

11. Which alliteratively named defensive end led the AFC in sacks after recording 13.5 of them in 1996?

12. The Seahawks won the AFC West title once in the 1990s. In what year?

13. Who was the starting quarterback in 15 of the 16 games in that division-winning season?

14. In 1998, which defensive lineman became the first Seahawk to win the NFL's Deacon Jones Award?

15. Which two Seahawks running backs went to the Pro Bowl during the 1990s?

16. Which wide receiver played in 71 straight games for the Seahawks between 1995 and 1999, catching at least one pass in each of them, before being traded to Dallas?

17. Which All-Pro linebacker led the team in tackles in 1997, 1998 and 1999?

18. Which quarterback had a starting record of 0-8 during the disastrous 1992 season?

19. What was the highest number of wins recorded by the Seahawks in a single season during the 1990s? a) 8 b) 9 c) 10

20. Which quarterback fumbled five times during a 1990 game against San Diego? a) Stan Gelbaugh b) Jeff Kemp c) Dave Krieg

Quiz 18: Answers

1. Green Bay 2. Kelcie McCray 3. University of Tulsa 4. True 5. Chuck Knox, Mike Holmgren and Pete Carroll 6. Minnesota 7. True 8. Blue 9. LA Rams and Buffalo Bills 10. Dave Krieg 11. Carolina 12. 31-14 13. 2004 14. Jim Zorn 15. Sam McCullum 16. Pete Gross 17. 2001 18. Charlie Rogers 19. c) Taima 20. a) Shaun Alexander

Quiz 20: 2000s

1. Seattle opened the new Seahawks Stadium in 2002 with a 24-13 loss to which NFC rival?

2. Who scored five touchdowns in the first half of a Sunday Night Football rout of the Vikings in 2002?

3. The Seahawks suffered a heart-breaking playoff loss in January 2004 to which team after Al Harris returned an interception 54 yards for the winning touchdown?

4. What team did the Seahawks face in Super Bowl XL?

5. What was the score in that game?

6. Who scored the Seahawks' only touchdown in Super Bowl XL?

7. True or false – The Seahawks won four straight NFC West titles in the middle of the 2000s?

8. True or false – The Giants missed three game-winning field goal attempts to gift the Seahawks a win in 2005?

9. Who was the only Seahawks quarterback elected to the Pro Bowl in the 2000s?

10. Who were the three Seattle defenders to record more than 10 sacks in a single regular season during the 2000s?

11. The Seahawks made their Super Bowl debut at which stadium?

12. Who were the four Seahawks quarterbacks to record a win as a starter between 2000 and 2009?

13. Which two quarterbacks started games for the Seahawks during the 2000s but failed to register a win?

14. In 2003, with the thermometers topping 98F, the Seahawks played the hottest game in franchise history. Which team did they beat in the heat 38-0?

15. Whose 6,445 receiving yards between 2000 and 2006 are good enough to put him third on the Seahawks all-time list?

16. Which alliteratively named running back rushed for 2,602 yards in a Seahawks career that ran from 2002 to 2008?

17. Which head coach's single season in charge in 2009 ended with a disappointing record of 5-11?

18. Who was the only Seattle defensive lineman to have been named a First-Team All-Pro during the decade?

19. Which team committed a then NFL record 11 false start penalties during a 24-21 loss to Seattle in 2005? a) Dallas b) NY Giants c) Philadelphia

20. In what year did the Seahawks change from silver to blue helmets? a) 2002 b) 2003 c) 2004

Quiz 19: Answers

1. Knox, Flores, Erickson and Holmgren 2. Cortez Kennedy 3. Warren Moon 4. Ken Behring 5. Paul Allen 6. Dennis Erickson 7. Denver 8. John Friesz 9. Todd Peterson 10. Derrick Fenner 11. Michael McCrary 12. 1999 13. Jon Kitna 14. Michael Sinclair 15. John L. Williams and Chris Warren 16. Joey Galloway 17. Chad Brown 18. Stan Gelbaugh 19. b) 9 20. c) Dave Krieg

Quiz 21: 2010 and Beyond

1. Who led the Seahawks in touchdowns every year from 2010 through to 2015?

2. Which team defeated Seattle in Super Bowl XLIX?

3. The Seahawks were involved in the third coldest game in NFL history in January 2016. Which team were they playing?

4. Who scored 101 and 99-yard kickoff return touchdowns in a 27-20 win over the Chargers in September 2010?

5. Despite taking the lead with just 31 seconds remaining the Seahawks suffered a heart-breaking 30-28 loss to which team in the 2012/13 Divisional Round playoff?

6. Who scored on a controversial last-second Hail Mary as the Seahawks beat the Packers 14-12 in October 2012?

7. True or false – The Seahawks were the first team to reach the playoffs with a losing regular season record?

8. The Seahawks reached Super Bowl XLIX after an amazing come from behind overtime win against which team?

9. Who scored the game-winning touchdown that took Seattle to Super Bowl XLIX?

10. Whose last-second interception broke Seattle hearts in Super Bowl XLIX?

11. Which defensive back recorded an interception in four successive games in the latter part of the 2011 season?

12. Before the Seahawks in mid 2010s what was the last team to play in back-to-back Super Bowls?

13. The Seahawks racked up a franchise-record 596 yards during a 35-6 rout of which division rival in December 2014?

14. Which three players had over 100 yards receiving in a single game during the 2016 season?

15. True or false – A car dealership gave away $420,000 in prizes after Seattle shut out the Giants in December 2013?

16. Who set a Seattle rookie record after rushing for 209 yards against the 49ers in November 2015?

17. The Seahawks rushed for a mammoth 350 yards in a 38-17 victory over which NFC rival in November 2014?

18. The Seattle defense restricted which divisional rival to just 13 rushing yards during a 2013 victory?

19. Between 2012 and 2013 the Seahawks won how many consecutive home games? a) 12 b) 13 c) 14

20. With which pick in the NFL Draft did the Seahawks select Russell Wilson? a) 65 b) 75 c) 85

Quiz 20: Answers

1. Arizona 2. Shaun Alexander 3. Green Bay 4. Pittsburgh 5. 21-10 6. Jerramy Stevens 7. True 8. True 9. Matt Hasselbeck 10. John Randle, Patrick Kerney and Julian Peterson 11. Ford Field 12. Kitna, Hasselbeck, Dilfer and Wallace 13. Brock Huard and Charlie Frye 14. Arizona 15. Darrell Jackson 16. Maurice Morris 17. Jim Mora Jr 18. Patrick Kerney 19. b) NY Giants 20. a) 2002

Quiz 22: Pot Luck

1. Which former Seahawks legend hosts a podcast called 'Finish The Game'?

2. Who was the first Seattle running back to rush for over 1,000 yards in a season?

3. Which defensive back intercepted two passes, forced two fumbles, recovered one of them and recorded 11 tackles in a 1993 win over Cleveland?

4. Who succeeded Tom Flores as Seattle head coach?

5. Which former Seahawk was elected into the US House of Representatives in November 1994?

6. Who tied an NFL record after recording an eighth kickoff return touchdown during a 2012 loss to Miami?

7. True or false – Russell Wilson was the first player to throw for over 300 yards and rush for over 100 yards in a game in NFL history?

8. Which future NFL head coach was the Seahawks' defensive coordinator from 2009 until 2012?

9. In the video to the hit song 'White Walls' rapper Macklemore wore a #96 jersey honoring which Seahawks defensive star?

10. In 2014, the Seahawks lost the loudest outdoor stadium record to which team?

11. True or false – In their first 40 seasons, the Seahawks had a regular season record of 315 wins and 313 losses?

12. Which multi-dimensional Raider holds the record for the most rushing yards in a game against the Seahawks after racking up 221 of them in a game in November 1987?

13. After 15 years in Minnesota, which Hall of Fame defensive lineman spent his 16th and final season in 1979 with the Seahawks?

14. Which linebacker returned fumbles for a touchdown a franchise record three times during a Seahawks career that ran from 1997 to 2004?

15. Who was Seattle's starting center in their Super Bowl XLVIII triumph?

16. The Seahawks combined with which AFC team to score just nine points during a surprise 6-3 loss in 2011?

17. True or false – Between 2010 and 2015 the Seahawks won 12 straight Thursday Night games?

18. Which fearsome defensive lineman holds the record for the most forced fumbles in franchise history with 28?

19. The Seahawks gave up a 99-yard touchdown pass to which team during a 1994 game? a) Denver b) Oakland c) San Diego

20. In 1992, the Seahawks set the NFL record for the fewest points scored in a full 16-game season. How many did they total? a) 140 b) 150 c) 160

Quiz 21: Answers
1. Marshawn Lynch 2. New England 3. Minnesota 4. Leon Washington 5. Atlanta 6. Golden Tate 7. True 8. Green Bay 9. Jermaine Kearse 10. Malcolm Butler 11. Brandon Browner 12. New England 13. Arizona 14. Doug Baldwin, Jimmy Graham and Tyler Lockett 15. True 16. Thomas Rawls 17. New York Giants 18. St Louis Rams 19. c) 14 20. b) 75

Quiz 23: The Numbers Game

What number jersey was worn by the following Seahawks players?

1. Norm Johnson and Jon Ryan

2. Marshawn Lynch and Shawn Springs

3. Steve Broussard and Kam Chancellor

4. Walter Jones and Brian Millard

5. Dave Krieg and John Friesz

6. Curt Warner and Michael Boulware

7. Brian Blades and Doug Baldwin

8. Cliff Avril and LeRoy Hill

9. Michael Bennett and Joe Nash

10. John L. Williams and Ricky Watters

11. K.J. Wright and Fredd Young

12. Jim Zorn and Paul Richardson

13. Dave Brown and C.J. Prosise

14. Shaun Alexander and Jeremy Lane

15. Earl Thomas and Dwayne Harper

16. Bruce Irvin and Lofa Tatupu

17. Steve Hutchinson and Russell Okung

18. Rick Mirer and Josh Brown

19. Bobby Engram and Joey Galloway

20. Leon Washington and Daryll Williams

Quiz 22: Answers

1. Shaun Alexander 2. Curt Warner 3. Eugene Robinson 4. Dennis Erickson 5. Steve Largent 6. Leon Washington 7. True 8. Gus Bradley 9. Cortez Kennedy 10. Kansas City 11. True 12. Bo Jackson 13. Carl Eller 14. Chad Brown 15. Max Unger 16. Cleveland 17. False 18. Jacob Green 19. C) San Diego 20. a) 140

Quiz 24: Pot Luck

1. Which defensive back's 90-yard interception return in the 2014 Divisional round playoff win against the Panthers is the longest in the postseason in franchise history?

2. Who intercepted a Colin Kaepernick pass in the final seconds of the NFC Championship to send the Seahawks to Super Bowl XLVIII?

3. Who famously tipped the pass that led to that historic pick?

4. The Seahawks played the first three home games of the 1994 season at what venue?

5. True or false – The Seahawks are the only team in the NFL never to have worn white jerseys in a home game?

6. Which opposition quarterback holds the record for the most passing yards in a single game against the Seahawks?

7. The Seahawks were defeated 30-14 by which divisional rival in their first Conference Championship game?

8. Curt Warner was the first Seattle back to rush for over 1,000 yards in successive seasons. Who was the second?

9. Which Hall of Famer spent the final year of his career with the Seahawks in 2004, catching 24 passes for 362 yards and three touchdowns?

10. Only three Seahawks had multiple interceptions during the 2016 regular season. Can you name them?

11. Which Seahawk received an unsportsmanlike conduct penalty against the Saints in 2016 for hugging the ref after he returned a fumble for a touchdown?

12. Walter Jones is one of just two Seattle o-linemen to have been named a First-Team All-Pro more than once while playing for the Seahawks. Which guard is the other?

13. Which quarterback holds the record for the most pass completions in franchise history?

14. True or false – The Seahawks won only one of their first six playoff games?

15. The Seahawks tied the NFL record by recording how many safeties during the 1993 regular season?

16. True or false – In their debut NFL season, the Seahawks scored just nine field goals?

17. Which Kansas City Chief recorded a record seven sacks during a 1990 game against the Seahawks?

18. Which hard-hitting linebacker returned two fumbles for touchdowns during the 2015 season?

19. What was the nickname of offensive tackle Howard Ballard? a) Home b) House c) Shack

20. What is the most wins that the Seahawks have recorded in a single regular season? a) 12 b) 13 c) 14

Quiz 23: Answers

1. #9 2. #24 3. #31 4. #71 5. #17 6. #28 7. #89 8. #56 9. #72 10. #32 11. #50 12. #10 13. #22 14. #37 15. #29 16. #51 17. #76 18. #3 19. #84 20. #33

Quiz 25: Anagrams 2

Rearrange the letters to make the name of a current or former Seahawks great.

1. Rows Unless III

2. Crasher Darn Him

3. Jots Renewal

4. Raw Current

5. Astral Home

6. Vegan Letters

7. Clearer Plot

8. Hen Alarm Clock

9. Test Me Backlash

10. A Keg Diver

11. Deny Rocket Zen

12. A Budding Owl

13. Grown By Babe

14. Nil Became Tenth

15. Crane Whirrs

16. Exam Rung

17. Defy Ground

18. Shut Cake Havens

19. Relax Nuns Ahead

20. Ribald Beans

Quiz 24: Answers

1. Kam Chancellor 2. Malcolm Smith 3. Richard Sherman 4. Husky Stadium 5. True 6. Ben Roethlisberger 7. LA Raiders 8. Chris Warren 9. Jerry Rice 10. Richard Sherman, Kam Chancellor and Earl Thomas 11. Earl Thomas 12. Steve Hutchinson 13. Matt Hasselbeck 14. True 15. 4 16. True 17. Derrick Thomas 18. Bobby Wagner 19. b) House 20. b) 13

16759214R00033

Made in the USA
San Bernardino, CA
18 December 2018